A History

FIONA BEDDALL

Level 3

Series Editors: Andy Hopkins and Jocelyn Potter

Pearson Education Limited
Edinburgh Gate, Harlow,
Essex CM20 2JE, England
and Associated Companies throughout the world.

ISBN-13: 978-1-4058-3350-9
ISBN-10: 1-4058-3350-5

This edition first published by Penguin Books 2006

3 5 7 9 10 8 6 4 2

Text copyright © Fiona Beddall 2006
Maps by Martin Sanders

Typeset by Graphicraft Limited, Hong Kong
Set in 11/14pt Bembo
Printed in China
SWTC/02

Produced for the Publishers by
Graphicraft Productions Limited, Dartford, UK

Published by Pearson Education Limited in association with
Penguin Books Ltd, both companies being subsidiaries of Pearson Plc

Acknowledgements
Every effort has been made to trace the copyright holders and we apologise in advance for an
unintentional omissions. We would be pleased to insert the appropriate acknowledgement in any
subsequent edition of this publication.

We are grateful to the following for permission to reproduce photographs:

akg-images Ltd: pg13 (©Sotheby's); **Corbis:** pg27 (Stapleton Collection); **Mary Evans:** pg33;
Popperfoto.com: pg9, pg20;

Picture Research by Sally Cole

For a complete list of the titles available in the Penguin Readers series please write to your local
Pearson Education office or to: Penguin Readers Marketing Department, Pearson Education,
Edinburgh Gate, Harlow, Essex, CM20 2JE

Contents

Introduction

In the 1930s, about a quarter of the world's population was ruled by the British. 'The sun never goes down on our empire,' they said. They meant that it was always daytime somewhere in the Empire. They also meant that their empire was for ever.

Of course, no empire is for ever. Britain lost its empire after the Second World War, but before that the British Empire was the largest in history.

This book tells Britain's story, from its days as part of the Roman Empire two thousand years ago. It describes the different groups of people who have lived there. It shows how the four countries of the United Kingdom – England, Scotland, Wales and Northern Ireland – came together as one state. And it explains the birth of Parliament and the battles for power between kings, religious groups and ordinary people.

It also tells the stories of some of the great, and not-so-great, men and women who shaped the British nation. In these pages you will find out how Henry VIII's love life brought a new religion to the people of England. You will meet Oliver Cromwell. He destroyed a king's power and then ruled England in his place. And you will learn about some of Britain's great queens. Boudica was a dangerous enemy to the Romans. Elizabeth I was a strong ruler who made England one of the most powerful countries in Europe. Victoria was Empress of India and Queen of Britain's lands around the world.

You will also find out about the ordinary men and women of British history. Some of them left Britain and built new lives across the seas in America, Australia and New Zealand. Others stayed in Britain, but life changed for them too. This book explains how Britain's past formed Britain today.

TIMELINE OF BRITAIN

England in the Roman Empire	**55 BC** Julius Caesar lands in Britain **60 AD** Boudica fights the Romans
Angles and Saxons control England	**793** The Vikings start attacking Britain
Viking kings control England	
Saxon kings of England	
Norman kings of England	⊠ **1066** The Battle of Hastings is won by William the Conqueror
Plantagenet kings of England	**1171** The Norman invasion of Ireland **1215** *Magna Carta* **1264** England's first parliament **1284** Wales loses independence from England
Tudor kings and queens of England	**1534** Henry VIII becomes head of the Church of England ⊠ **1588** The Spanish invasion of Britain fails
Stuart kings of England and Scotland	**1620** The *Mayflower* sails to New England **1649** War between Charles I and Parliament ends in Charles's death
Rule of Oliver Cromwell	
Stuart kings and queens of England and Scotland	**1688** James II leaves England to William of Orange **1707** Scotland joins England and Wales as one state
Parliament controls Britain	**1756** The East India Company wins control of Bengal **1771** Britain's first factory **1776** American independence ⊠ **1805** Britain rules the seas after the Battle of Trafalgar ⊠ **1815** Napoleon is finally defeated in the Battle of Waterloo **1876** Queen Victoria becomes Empress of India **1914–1918** First World War **1922** Independence for Southern Ireland **1939–1945** Second World War **1947** Indian independence **1997** Hong Kong returns to China

Chapter 1   Invaders

It was 1066, and Edward, King of England, was dead. He had no children. The most important people in the country met to choose a new king. They chose Harold. Harold wasn't a blood relative of King Edward, but he was the Queen's brother. He was a popular man for the job.

But other powerful men wanted to be king too. One of them was the King of Norway, Harold Hardrada, and a few months after King Edward's death his army invaded the north of England. King Harold of England went north, defeated the invaders and killed King Harold of Norway. But three days later, there was more bad news.

William of Normandy (in the north of France) was on the south coast of England with an army. 'Before King Edward died, he chose me as the next king,' he said. Perhaps this was true. Edward's mother was a Norman, and Edward lived in Normandy as a child. He preferred Normans to the people of England. So Harold raced south with his army. William was waiting for him at Hastings. At the end of the battle, Harold was dead and William of Normandy was William the Conqueror, King of England.

Roman Britain

The Normans weren't the first people who invaded Britain. In 55 BC* the great Roman Julius Caesar brought an army across the sea from France. For four hundred years, England was part of the Roman Empire. When the Romans first arrived, there were many different groups of people. Each group had its own king. They didn't think of themselves as 'British', but the Romans called the people from all these groups 'Britons'.

* BC/AD: years before/after the birth of Christ

Boudica

The Romans tried many times to conquer the areas of Britain that we now call Wales and Scotland. But they never kept control there. In the rest of Britain, the local people were much easier to control. But Boudica was different.

Her husband was a local king in the east of England. When he died in 60AD, the Romans tried to take all his money. Roman soldiers attacked Boudica and her daughters. Boudica was angry.

Soon she had an army of Britons behind her. They attacked Colchester, London and St Albans – the three most important cities in Britain at that time – and destroyed them completely. But in the end, the Romans defeated her. There is a story that her body lies under London's most famous railway station, King's Cross.

In many places around the country you can still see the straight roads, strong walls and fine houses that the Romans built. In the new Roman towns, Britons started to live like Romans. They wore Roman clothes and went to the theatre and the baths. Most townspeople could speak Latin. Many could read and write it too. In the later years of Roman rule they became Christian.

The Angles and Saxons

But in 409 the Roman army left Britain to fight in other parts of the Empire. Soon after this, invaders from present-day Germany and Denmark, the Angles and Saxons, came to Britain.

The Angle and Saxon armies destroyed everything in their path, and the Roman way of life disappeared from Britain. Many Britons moved west to escape the invaders. By the 7th century, groups of Britons were in control of present-day Scotland, Wales and Cornwall, but Angles and Saxons ruled the rest of Britain. People started to call this area 'Angle-land'. Later its name became 'England'.

The Vikings

Then, at the end of the 8th century, new invaders started attacking the coasts of Britain – Vikings from Scandinavia. At first they came to steal gold and silver from monasteries. Then some made their homes in Britain, and from the 860s they controlled a large area of northern and eastern England. The Saxon kings fought against them. Alfred the Great defeated the Vikings and sent them away from Britain. But they returned, and in the early 11th century there was a Viking king of England, King Cnut.

The Normans

The Normans came next. Their conquest was probably the most important in British history because it was the last.

Since 1066 and the Battle of Hastings, many people have moved to Britain from other countries. For example, a lot of French and Dutch Protestants* arrived in the 17th century to escape problems with the Catholics* in their homelands. And in the 20th century large numbers of people came from India, the Caribbean and other places that were in the British Empire. But no foreign army has conquered Britain since the Normans.

William the Conqueror had to fight other Saxon armies in England after Harold was defeated. But then he was able to build a new, Norman England. By 1068, he owned all the land. He asked his Norman friends to look after it for him. They made money from the farmland and paid some of it to the king. They

---

* Protestants, Catholics: people who belong to different Christian groups

3

also used the money to pay for Norman soldiers. Each Norman lord built a home with strong, high walls and lived there with his private army. The Saxons owned nothing. They belonged to the Norman lords.

For more than two hundred years the language of government and literature was the Normans' language, French. The Saxons continued to speak their own language, Anglo-Saxon, with some Scandinavian words. The Saxons' language finally grew into modern English, but as a result of the Norman invasion, half the words in today's English language come from French.

Chapter 2   The United Kingdom

England is a country but it isn't a state. It is part of a state called 'The United Kingdom of Great Britain and Northern Ireland'. This name is less than a hundred years old, but English rule in other parts of the United Kingdom started soon after the time of William the Conqueror.

Wales

When England was safely under their control, the Normans started the conquest of Wales. The conquest was completed by William the Conqueror's son. There were a few years of independence in the 12th and 13th centuries, but since 1284 the rulers of England have also ruled in Wales. The Welsh language is still spoken by half a million people.

Scotland

Scotland stayed independent much longer than Wales – until the end of the 13th century, when it was conquered by the English king, Edward I. But thirty years later it became independent

4

The United Kingdom

SCOTLAND

Atlantic Ocean

Edinburgh

NORTHERN
IRELAND

North Sea

Belfast

Irish Sea

Leeds

REPUBLIC
OF IRELAND

Dublin

Manchester

ENGLAND

Birmingham

WALES

Stratford-
upon-Avon

Cardiff

London

Lewes

Hastings

CORNWALL

250 km

again. England and Scotland finally came together in 1603. Queen Elizabeth I of England died without children, and her nearest relative was James, King of Scotland. During the next century the two countries had the same kings and queens, but different parliaments and laws.

Twice in that time, the English parliament chose a new king for both countries. The Scots were very angry. Some wanted war with their more powerful neighbour. But others saw a better future. England was growing rich from its empire abroad. Scotland was failing to build its own empire. So Scotland should join England, and as one country they could enjoy the empire together.

The English liked this idea, but the Scots weren't so sure. Finally, in 1707, the Scottish parliament voted to join England. (Many Scottish politicians were paid to vote this way.) Scotland lost its own parliament and the Scottish politicians moved south to London. England, Scotland and Wales were now one state: Great Britain.

When Scotland joined England, the two countries' differences didn't just disappear. In 1715, and again in 1745, people from the Highlands, in the northwest of Scotland, and from other areas fought to have a new king. They were defeated both times. In 1745, the English destroyed complete villages. Many people were killed, and the 'lucky' ones were sent abroad.

The Scots never fought the English again. By the end of the 18th century, they were joining the British army in large numbers and playing an important part in the government of the British Empire.

Ireland

Ireland's story was very different. Ireland was first conquered by an army from Britain in 1171. The Irish finally won independence for most of their island in 1922. In all that time,

British rule brought Ireland very little money and a lot of trouble.

The Norman invasion of Ireland in 1171 was the idea of an Irish king, Dermot of Leinster. When he stole another king's wife, he lost power over his lands. He asked the English king, Henry II, for help. Henry sent an army, and the island of Ireland has never been completely independent since then.

Henry II

Henry II became King of England because of his Norman mother. He was the first king from the Plantagenet family that ruled England after the Normans. He also ruled the French lands of his wife and his father. At its greatest, his empire reached from Ireland to the Pyrenees, mountains in the south-west of France. The kings of England continued to rule lands in France until 1557.

Norman lords ruled the area around Dublin, and most of the time they were independent of the government in England. Irish kings continued to control the rest of the country. Little changed until the 16th century, when most people in Britain became Protestant. Most Irish people stayed Catholic. The Catholics tried to push the Protestants out of Ireland, but they failed. In 1607, the last Catholic lords left the country and, for the first time, all of Ireland was controlled by England.

The Protestant rulers of England wanted to make Ireland less Catholic. So they decided to send large numbers of Scottish Protestants there. Most of these Scots made their home in the north of Ireland, and their families still live there today.

The Irish Catholics didn't like the Protestants in the north or the English government. In every British war of the

17th century, the Catholics fought for the side that lost. As a punishment, Catholics in the early 18th century couldn't own land, or even a good horse. There was an Irish parliament, but Catholics couldn't vote or be politicians. And they couldn't go to university. Irish Catholics became very poor, and the rich Protestant landowners weren't interested in their problems. Some of the laws against Catholics were changed after a few years, but too little was done too late.

In 1798, the Irish fought unsuccessfully for independence from England. After this, the English decided to end the Irish parliament. Irish politicians, like the Scots before them, moved to London. There, they joined the parliament of a state that was now called the United Kingdom of Great Britain and Ireland.

Most Catholics in Ireland ate little except the potatoes that they grew on their very small farms. In the 1840s, potatoes failed to grow in Europe. In most countries this was not a serious problem, because there was other food. But in Ireland the result was terrible. People started to die. The British government did very little to help. The Church of England offered free food, but only to people who became Protestant. Of a population of eight and a half million, about one million died and another million went abroad, most of them to the US.

The Catholic dream of an independent Ireland continued. After battles in Parliament and in the streets of Irish cities, independence finally came in 1922. But the Protestants in the north refused to be part of a Catholic Irish state. So Ireland was cut in two. Northern Ireland continued to be part of the United Kingdom.

Northern Ireland

About 35% of the people in Northern Ireland were Catholic. They wanted to be part of the independent state of Ireland.

Stones are thrown at police in Northern Ireland in 1969.

The Protestants were afraid of the Catholics, so they controlled the votes for politicians unfairly. They also kept the best jobs and houses for themselves. In the 1960s, Catholic demonstrations were stopped violently. So the British government sent their army to protect the Catholics.

But Catholics didn't want the British army in their country. A Catholic group, the IRA, started to fight for independence from Britain in the north. When the first IRA fighter shot a British soldier, many Catholics were pleased. The IRA killed British soldiers and Protestant policemen and politicians. Later they killed anyone who was Protestant or British. Catholic violence was answered with more violence by the British army and the Protestant Irish. Terrible things were done by all sides, but perhaps the worst violence has now passed. In the last few years, IRA activity has stopped. Many Catholic and Protestant politicians, and the British and Irish governments, are trying to build a Northern Ireland which is free of violence and fair for all.

National parliaments

The Welsh and Scots haven't fought battles against the English for many centuries, but the idea of independence from England never really died. England is the biggest of the four countries in the United Kingdom, so it has the largest number of politicians in the parliament in London. Many people in Wales, Scotland and Northern Ireland felt that the London parliament didn't do enough for them. In the 1990s, the Scots, Welsh and Northern Irish were given their own parliaments. They still have politicians in London, but they have others in their own capitals: Edinburgh, Cardiff and Belfast. These national parliaments make some decisions, for example about schools and hospitals, but tax, the army and other important matters are still controlled from London.

Chapter 3   God and Government

Henry VIII was king of England in the early 16th century. He was handsome and clever. He loved sport, music and dance. No king was ever more popular with his people.

But he was worried. He didn't have a son to follow him as King. In the half-century before Henry's rule, England suffered terribly as two families fought for control of the country. Now these wars were finished and Henry's family, the Tudors, were in control. But the wars could easily start again after his death. For Henry, a son was very important – more important even than his people's religion.

Catholic Britain

From the 7th century, almost everyone in Britain was a Roman Catholic. By the time of Henry VIII, the Catholic Church was very powerful. In those days, only a few people reached the age of fifty. Life after death was very important to them, and for this they needed the Church. Even the poorest farmers gave the Church 10% of the food that they produced. They also worked on Church land without payment. Rich families gave large amounts of money. Everyone believed that they were buying a better life after death. The Church became very rich – much richer than the King of England.

Henry VIII: two women, two churches

Katharine of Aragon was a Spanish princess. She was married to Henry's older brother. He died young and Henry, as the future king, decided to marry Katharine. She was useful to England because Spain was one of the most powerful countries in Europe.

A Christian couldn't usually marry his brother's wife, but the head of the Catholic Church, the Pope, gave special permission.

Henry VIII and Katharine of Aragon had only one child – a daughter, Mary. When no son came, Henry looked for a reason. He decided that his marriage to his brother's wife was wrong. As a punishment, he and Katharine had no sons.

Henry was always interested in other women, but now he fell completely in love with a young Englishwoman, Anne Boleyn. She was much younger than Katharine. She was clever and funny and maybe she could give Henry a son.

Henry sent his assistant, Thomas Wolsey, to Rome to ask the Pope for an end to his marriage with Katharine. But the Pope was the prisoner of one of Katharine's relatives. He couldn't agree to Henry's request.

Wolsey went back to England and told his king the bad news. Henry was very angry. He put Wolsey in prison. Then he made a decision that changed Britain for ever. The Pope was head of the Catholic Church, and he was being difficult. So in 1534, Henry closed the Catholic Church and started a new one, the Church of England, with a new head – the king. A few politicians and priests spoke in disagreement against this, so Henry cut off their heads.

Henry was the writer of a book which attacked the religious ideas of the Protestants. But now his new church followed these Protestant ideas. The Bible* was read in English in church, not in Latin, and there were no pictures in church of anyone except Jesus. For people in the 16th century, these changes were very serious. But to Henry they didn't matter, because he was only interested in one thing. His new church gave him permission to end his marriage with Katharine. Then he married Anne Boleyn.

Henry soon realised that his power as head of the Church was useful in other ways. He needed money, and the Church had lots

* Bible: the religious book of the Christian Church

King Henry VIII

of it. Monasteries owned large areas of land, and gold and silver too. So he decided to close them. Henry took everything. Many beautiful buildings were destroyed, and 11,000 religious men and women suddenly lost their homes. You can still see the broken walls of old monasteries in many parts of Britain today.

Henry's other wives

Sadly for Henry, his new church didn't solve his marriage problems. When Anne Boleyn gave Henry a daughter, Elizabeth, but no son, he cut off her head. He finally had a son with his third wife, Jane Seymour, but she died after the birth of the baby.

His fourth wife was Anne of Cleves, a German princess who he chose from a picture. In real life she was very ugly, and he ended their marriage after six months. He didn't make the same mistake again. Catherine Howard was a beautiful English girl of sixteen when she married Henry, a fat 49-year-old. But Henry learnt that she had a lover. He cut off her head. His sixth wife, Catherine Parr, was luckier than the rest: Henry died before her.

Edward VI

After Henry VIII's death, his nine-year-old son became king. Edward VI was an unhealthy but very intelligent boy, and he had strong ideas about religion. He started to make England even more Protestant than under his father. But he only lived to the age of fifteen. There was nobody who could become the next king. So Edward's older sister Mary became queen.

Mary I

Mary, Katharine of Aragon's Catholic daughter, threw out all the Protestant changes that were introduced by her father and brother. Most people in England were happy about this. They didn't like Protestant ideas very much. But then Mary killed lots of Protestants. In three years, 280 men and women were burned in front of crowds of people. Mary became very unpopular.

She was thirty-eight and unmarried when she became queen. She hated the idea of Anne Boleyn's Protestant daughter, Elizabeth, as the next queen, so she really wanted a child. She married King Philip of Spain. Twice she thought she was having his baby. But she had a stomach problem – and it killed her. The return of the Catholic Church in England died with her.

Elizabeth I

When Mary's sister Elizabeth became queen, she tried to find a middle way for religion. She wanted a Church of England that Protestants and Catholics could accept. But this was impossible.

First, the Puritans didn't like it. The Puritans were Protestants who wanted simple churches and simple clothes for their priests. To them, the Church of England wasn't different enough from the Catholic Church. And they didn't want the Queen as head of the Church. Elizabeth thought that their ideas were dangerous. Many Puritans were put in prison or killed.

Second, the Catholics didn't like it. The Pope told the people of the Catholic Church to end Elizabeth's rule. 'Henry VIII's marriage to her mother, Anne Boleyn, was wrong,' he said. He secretly sent European priests to England to start a Catholic war against the Queen. So Elizabeth made Catholicism against the law. People had to pay lots of money if they didn't go to a Protestant church on Sunday. Lots of Catholics were put in prison, and a few were killed. Catholic priests continued to travel around the country secretly, but it was very dangerous. There are still many big 16th-century houses in England with 'priest holes' – secret places for Catholic priests to hide.

Mary Queen of Scots

Elizabeth's closest relative was her Catholic cousin, Mary Queen of Scots. In 1567, Mary made the people of Scotland very angry when she married her husband's murderer. She had to escape to England, leaving her baby son James as king of Scotland. Elizabeth wanted to make her welcome. But to Catholics, Mary was the true queen of England, because Henry VIII's second marriage wasn't real. So Elizabeth had even more problems with her Catholic enemies. Mary lived as a prisoner in England for nineteen years. Finally, Elizabeth's spies proved that Mary was making plans against Elizabeth. Elizabeth sadly ordered her death.

William Shakespeare

Elizabeth's rule was a time of danger for some, but many other people enjoyed life. Plays became very popular, and England's first real theatre was built. The greatest writer for the theatre was William Shakespeare. His father was an ordinary trader and he only went to school, in Stratford-upon-Avon, until the age of fourteen. Later he worked in London as a writer and an actor. Some of his thirty-seven plays were watched by the Queen at her palace, and they are still enjoyed around the world today.

The Spanish attack England

The next danger for Protestant England came from the most powerful country in Europe: Spain. In 1588, the Spanish king, Mary I's husband Philip, sent 27,000 men in 130 ships to the English coast. England had little hope of defeating them.

Philip's ships tried to join a Spanish army from the Netherlands. But luckily for England, the wind, and an attack by English boats, made this impossible. The Spanish ships were defeated and decided to return home. But they hit a terrible storm, and half the Spanish ships were destroyed.

Spain and the Catholics lost some of their power in Europe and England continued to be a Protestant country. When Elizabeth died in 1603, after forty-five years as queen, most of her people were strongly Protestant.

Religion after Elizabeth

Later in the 17th century, Britain had a Catholic king, James II. But by then it was impossible to bring the people of Britain back to the Catholic Church. After only three years, he had to leave Britain and a new, Protestant king was chosen.

Today, Christianity doesn't have the same importance in Britain that it had in earlier centuries. The numbers of Muslims, Hindus and Sikhs are growing, and a large part of the population doesn't believe in God. But there are still many more people in the Church of England than in the Catholic Church.

Chapter 4   Parliament against King

When Elizabeth I died without children, James Stuart, the Protestant son of Mary Queen of Scots, became king. He was already King James VI of Scotland. In 1603 he moved south to London as James I of England.

James discovered that English and Scottish parliaments had very different ideas about their powers. In Scotland, Parliament passed any laws that the king wanted. In England, Parliament wanted to make decisions too. This made James's rule very difficult, and brought even more trouble to his son. An important battle for control of the country was beginning.

The Magna Carta

James wasn't the first king who disagreed with his people about his powers. Back in the 13th century, King John had similar problems. But in those days there was no parliament.

John wasn't a strong ruler. He started his rule with an empire in France, but he soon lost most of his French lands – even Normandy. His lords chose this time to put controls on the power of the king. In 1215, with armies behind them, the lords told King John to agree to the *Magna Carta* – a list of rules for good government. For example, the state couldn't put someone in prison without a good reason. Under the *Magna Carta*, even the king had to follow the law. John didn't want to sign the *Magna Carta*. In the end he did, but he broke its rules almost immediately. The lords attacked him with their armies. Before he was defeated, John died.

Early parliaments

John's nine-year-old son became King Henry III and the lords went home. But then, as an adult, Henry decided to start an expensive war in Sicily (now in the south of Italy). The lords worried that he was becoming like his father, John. He was interested only in power and not in his people. They decided to ask Henry for a parliament of priests, lords, and ordinary landowners and businessmen. Without the agreement of this parliament, the King couldn't have tax money for his Sicilian war. (This idea of a parliament was very new, tried before only on the Isle of Man, a small island between Britain and Ireland.) The King refused to accept a parliament. So there was war closer to home.

The lords defeated King Henry at the Battle of Lewes (in the south of England) in 1264. Henry and his son, Prince Edward, were taken prisoner. For the next 18 months England was ruled by a parliament. But Prince Edward escaped, formed an army and defeated the lords. King Henry was in control again.

Parliament lost much of its power, but it didn't disappear. When Prince Edward became King Edward I, he needed money for his wars in Scotland. Higher taxes were more acceptable to the people when they were agreed by a people's parliament.

Slowly, over the next few centuries, Parliament started to vote for and against new laws too. But it was nearly 400 years before parliament had as much power as in 1264.

Charles I

When James I died in 1625, his son Charles became king. Charles I made the problems between king and parliament even worse. He started a very unsuccessful war against the Catholic countries Spain and France. Parliament tried to stop Charles's unfair taxes for the war, so Charles closed Parliament. He ruled without it for the next eleven years.

Without a parliament, Charles couldn't have his people's tax money. He found other, unfair and unpopular, ways to get money. Then, when Charles made changes to the Church of Scotland, violent demonstrations started in Scottish cities. Charles didn't have enough money for an army to stop the demonstrations. So he had to have a parliament again.

This new parliament didn't act as the king wanted. So Charles closed it after only three weeks. Charles fought the Scots with men who weren't professional soldiers. The Scots won, and took control of a large part of the north of England. Charles had to have another parliament.

Oliver Cromwell

This parliament stopped Charles's unfair taxes. But Charles needed soldiers again when there was violence between Catholics and Protestants in Northern Ireland. The politicians were worried. 'Maybe the king will use the soldiers against us,' they thought. So they passed a law that Parliament, not the king, was now in control of the country. And that meant war.

King and Parliament at war

In many families, brother fought brother and father fought son. The King's men won the first battle, but four years later, Charles I was defeated by Parliament and its army.

Parliament couldn't agree what they should do next. But in the end a court of law decided that Charles was an enemy of the people. In 1649, he was killed in front of a large crowd. His son, Charles II, was made king in Scotland, but Parliament soon defeated the Scots. Charles II had to escape to the Netherlands, leaving Parliament and the officers of its army in control of Britain.

Oliver Cromwell

Oliver Cromwell was an officer who fought for Parliament against the King. He introduced new ideas to his army and turned his men into excellent professional soldiers. At the end of the war, he was the most powerful man in Britain. Parliament offered him the title 'King'. Cromwell refused it, preferring the title 'Lord Protector'. But for eight years he ruled the country like the kings before him. Cromwell was a Puritan, so he disliked music and dance. Soon all the theatres were closed. Even Christmas was against the law.

The return of the King

When Cromwell died, his son became Lord Protector. But he wasn't a strong ruler and he couldn't control the army. So a group of politicians invited Charles II to return home.

Most people were very pleased to have Charles II as king. But Charles didn't like Parliament, and for most of his time as king he ruled without it. That meant no tax money, so he used money from the King of France.

Britain's last Catholic king

Charles II and his wife had no children. When Charles died in 1685, his Catholic brother James became king. James II started giving all the important jobs in the army and the universities to Catholics. He tried to get Catholics into Parliament. This was a bad idea because Catholics were hated by most of the population.

In 1688, a group of politicians invited Prince William of Orange, the Protestant Dutch husband (and cousin) of James's daughter Mary, to bring his army to England. When James's own army joined Prince William, James escaped to France.

A new law for kings and queens

Parliament was tired of kings who ruled without them. William and his wife Mary were asked to be king and queen. But first they had to agree to a new law. There could be no taxes, no army and no new laws without the agreement of Parliament. Politicians were now chosen every three years. And no Catholic could ever become king or queen.

William and Mary agreed to Parliament's new law. But the law didn't give Parliament all the power that some politicians were hoping for. William was a strong king who didn't leave the important decisions of government to Parliament.

Parliament didn't have to wait long for more power. William and Mary had no children, so Mary's sister Anne became queen after them. But when all Anne's children died young, there was a serious problem. Who could rule Britain after Anne?

There was only one possible person who wasn't Catholic: the German grandson of James I's daughter. He didn't speak English and he didn't like Britain. But when Anne died in 1714, he became King George I. For Parliament, George I was the perfect king. He wasn't interested in Britain, so Parliament was left in control of the country. And Parliament was careful that it never lost its power again. After 1714, the important decisions were made by politicians. Today's queen, Elizabeth II, is from the same family as George I. She is Britain's head of state, but she has no real power.

Chapter 5   Power to the People

From the 15th century, ordinary people had the same protection under the law as lords. But nobody imagined that ordinary workers had any real power. Only people with money could vote for politicians or join Parliament. Poor people did what they were told.

But then, in the late 18th century, Britain began to change. Historians now call the changes 'revolutions' because they were so important. There were new types of job, new towns and new ways to travel. And there were also new powers and protections for the ordinary workers of Britain.

Revolution in the country

Until the 19th century, most people in Britain worked on the land. They grew plants for food and kept farm animals. They produced butter and cheese. And in their homes they turned sheep's wool into cloth. English cloth was popular everywhere in Europe.

Farmers couldn't use all their fields every year. After a few years, the plants became unhealthy, so they left the field empty for a year. But in the 18th century, people found new ways to grow food. Farmers never had to leave a field empty, so they could produce more food.

The new ideas for farms could only work on large areas of land, and most farmers had small areas in different fields. In the second half of the 18th century, the government agreed to give a lot of land to the most powerful landowners. Many poorer farmers were left with nothing.

Revolution in towns

Also in the 18th century, there were changes in the cloth-making business. New machines helped to make cloth much faster than before. The machines were too big to keep at home. The world's first factories were built.

These factories employed many of the farmers who lost their land to the big landowners. Soon large towns grew around the factories. Manchester and Leeds, for example, grew in this way.

The factories made cloth from local wool, and also from American cotton. British cloth became even more popular in Europe than before. When the French Emperor Napoleon, Britain's great enemy, invaded Russia, his soldiers were wearing coats of British cloth.

British factories were soon copied in other European countries and their empires, and the world changed for ever. But these wonderful new machines didn't help the ordinary people of Britain.

Brunel

Many new roads, waterways and bridges were made in the 18th century. Then, in 1804, the world's first railway was built. Britain's greatest railway builder was Isambard Kingdom Brunel. He built more than 1,600 kilometres of railway line. His trains were faster, and his stations and bridges were more beautiful, than any others. He changed not only train travel, but also travel across the Atlantic Ocean. He built the first metal passenger ship, and another ship that was six times bigger than any other ship at that time.

Many factory owners in the late 18th and early 19th century controlled their workers' lives in a similar way to the Norman lords 700 years earlier. Workers weren't paid with money, but with cards that were only accepted in the factory shop. Adults were paid too little to feed a family. So their children worked in the factory too, some for eighteen hours a day, and there were a lot of accidents. The factory owners built houses for their workers, but most of these were cheap and small, with no clean water. Illness travelled quickly through the new towns.

The factory owners grew richer and richer. But their workers got no more money when the factory was successful. If workers started a trade union, they lost their jobs. If they refused to work, they weren't paid. Then their families had no food.

Better laws for workers

Workers became very angry. There were a lot of demonstrations, and some people wanted a violent British revolution like the revolution of 1789 in France. It was difficult for workers to change things in any other way. Ordinary workers didn't own their own houses, so they couldn't vote. Some cities, like Manchester and Birmingham, had no politicians because they were too new. But old towns with small populations had two politicians. It was very unfair.

Politicians didn't want a revolution, so they slowly gave workers more control over their lives. After a change in the law in 1825, workers could finally form trade unions. In 1832, the new cities got their own politicians and more men could vote. Children's hours of work were also controlled in the 1830s, and the Government offered children a few hours a day of free school lessons. From 1870, all children had to go to school. Child workers disappeared from British factories.

Votes for all

In the 19th century, more and more men were given the vote, but women still had no power. The Suffragettes were a group of women who wanted to change this. In the early 20th century they went on violent demonstrations. They shouted at politicians in Parliament. In prison, they refused to eat. One woman was killed when she threw herself under the King's horse during a race. But when the First World War started in 1914, these women stopped fighting the Government. They did the jobs of the men who were away at war. When the war ended, some women over the age of 30 and all men over the age of 21 could vote. Finally, in 1928, the rules for women and men became the same.

An end to poverty

Workers' lives at the end of the 19th century were a little better than a hundred years before. But when, in 1899, new soldiers were needed for a war in South Africa, large numbers of young

Working-class homes in 19th century London.

men were too unhealthy for the army. The Government decided to do more for the poor of Britain. In 1906, pay was introduced for people who couldn't work as a result of illness or old age. It was a small amount, but it was something.

After the Second World War ended in 1945, there was more money from the Government for old people. There was also money for families with children and for people who couldn't find work. Schools, hospitals, doctors and dentists were – and still are – free. Britain was the first state to protect its people in this way. Taxpayers have to pay for it, of course. But people are protected from the terrible poverty and unhealthy lives of earlier centuries.

Chapter 6   Britain's Great Empire

In the 1930s, about a quarter of the world's population was ruled by the British. 'The sun never goes down on our empire,' they said. They meant that it was always daytime somewhere in the Empire. They also meant that their empire was for ever. Perhaps they didn't remember the history of their first empire, an empire that was lost more than 150 years earlier.

British America

The religious enemies of Britain's rulers had the first successes of empire. In 1620, a group of English Puritans sailed to America in a boat called the *Mayflower*. They wanted to practise their religion freely and openly, and this was impossible in England. They built homes on the east coast of America, in an area that they called New England. Their first winter was very hard and more than half of them died. The rest escaped death only because they had help from the local people.

In the next few years, many people followed them across the Atlantic: Puritans and Catholics for religious reasons, and businessmen who were interested in trade. By the middle of the 18th century, there were 1.6 million British people living in North America. Then, in 1763, Britain defeated France in the Seven Years' War and won control of Canada too.

Sometimes there were attacks by the local American Indians, so the British Americans needed protection. The British government in London wanted taxes from the Americans to pay for an army. But the Americans had no politicians in Parliament, so to them the taxes were unlawful. In 1776 they decided to become independent from Britain. Five years of war followed. Finally, the British accepted that the US was an independent country. Only Canada continued to be British.

The British in India

On the other side of the world, there was better news for the British Empire.

In the 17th century a private English company, the East India Company, controlled a few ports on the west coast of India. To protect their trade interests in times of war, the East India Company employed an army of English officers and Indian men. In 1756 the ruler of Bengal, in north-east India, attacked British soldiers in his capital, Calcutta. He put many of them in prison overnight, but the prison didn't have enough air. In the morning, most of the soldiers were dead. The British called this prison the 'Black Hole of Calcutta'. They sent an army to defeat the Bengali ruler. From this time the real ruler of Bengal was the East India Company.

Slowly, other Indian states came under British control. By the middle of the 19th century, all India was part of the British Empire.

The British Empire was also growing in other parts of the world. Criminals were sent abroad because it was cheaper than prison. They went to America before it became independent. Then, from 1788, they were sent in large numbers to Australia. Soon other people were making their homes there too, and in New Zealand and Canada. If the local people – the Aborigines, Maoris and American Indians – were lucky, they only lost their land. If they were unlucky, they were killed.

The area around Cape Town in the south of Africa became British in 1806 after a war with the Dutch. It was a useful place because it was halfway on a ship's journey between Britain and India. Egypt was another useful part of Africa, between Europe and Asia. Napoleon and his French army invaded Egypt in 1798 but the British, under Horatio Nelson, destroyed most of Napoleon's ships in a battle on the River Nile.

Horatio Nelson

British success in 19th-century trade and empire was only possible because Britain ruled the seas. This control was mainly the result of the sea battles of Horatio Nelson. Nelson lost an arm in battle and he could only see out of one eye. But he knew how to defeat enemy warships.

After his success in Egypt, he fought the French and Spanish at the Battle of Trafalgar (1805). Nelson was killed in the battle, but most of the enemy ships were destroyed, and Britain's sea power was made safe for the next hundred years.

The central point of London today is Trafalgar Square, with Nelson in the middle, made of stone.

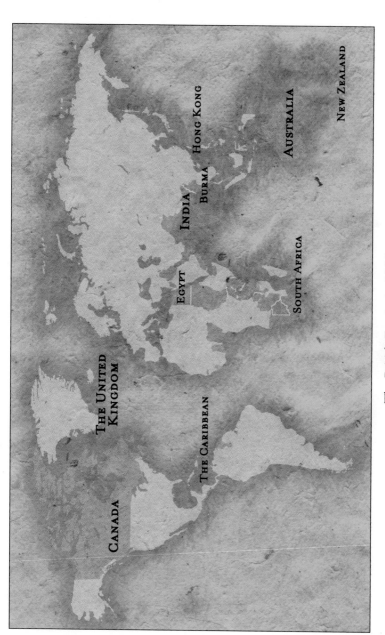

The British Empire in 1930

The war against Napoleon

Napoleon had more success in his battles on land than at sea. Soon he controlled a large part of Europe. He planned an invasion of Britain, but then he changed his mind and invaded Russia – a big mistake. He lost three-quarters of the 450,000 soldiers who went with him. At the same time, the British army pushed his soldiers out of Spain and Portugal. Finally, in 1815, he was defeated by Britain and Prussia★ at the Battle of Waterloo.

Empire in Africa

France and Britain continued to build their empires, in Asia and in Africa. Other European countries – Italy, Germany, Belgium – joined them in a race to rule Africa. The British fought for a long time against the African Zulus and the Dutch-speaking white Boers for control of South Africa and its gold. They moved north from there, and south from Egypt, until they controlled land from the top to the bottom of Africa.

Queen Victoria

Victoria became queen in 1837, at the age of eighteen. She had little real power over the world's most powerful country, but politicians listened to her strong opinions. She loved the idea of empire and she was pleased with the title 'Empress of India'. She was the mother of nine children and the grandmother of most of the kings and queens of Europe. When she died in 1901, very few people remembered a time before the Victorian Age.

★ Prussia: a large country with lands that are now in Germany, Poland and Lithuania

Queen Victoria

The First World War

By the early years of the 20th century, Germany, not France, was Britain's biggest enemy. German factories were becoming more successful than British ones, and the Germans were starting to build a lot of warships. The British didn't want to lose their control of the seas. They started a race to build more warships.

At that time the countries of Europe were grouping together for protection against their enemies: France and Russia against Germany, Austria–Hungary and Italy. The British decided to join with France and Russia. When the future emperor of Austria was murdered by the Serbs in 1914, the Russians joined the Serbs in war against the Austrians. This was the start of the First World War.

People from Britain and the Empire fought against the Germans in Belgium and the north of France, and against the Turks in Gallipoli (north-west Turkey). It was a new type of war. Nobody knew how to defeat enemy machine guns. The numbers of dead went higher and higher. On a single day in 1916, 20,000 British soldiers were killed. In the end, the Americans fought with the British, and the Germans and Austrians were defeated. But there were no real winners in this terrible war.

The 1920s and 1930s

Lands from the German and Turkish empires became British, but there was trouble after the war in other parts of the Empire. Much of Ireland became independent and India wanted independence too. Japan's power in Asia was growing. Were the British areas of Asia safe?

Britain wasn't as rich as before the war. In the 1930s, many factories closed and workers lost their jobs. A lot of people were unable to feed their families. When Adolf Hitler came to power in Germany, the British didn't want another war. There wasn't enough money for a strong British army. And Hitler only wanted land that Germany lost after the First World War.

But Hitler wanted more and more land. When he took control of Austria and Czechoslovakia (now the Czech Republic and Slovakia), the British did nothing. But it became clear that he was a danger to all Europeans. There were stories that he was sending large numbers of German Jews to prison for no reason. When he invaded Poland in 1939, the Second World War began.

The Second World War

At first the war went badly for Britain. British soldiers went to France, but they were soon pushed out again by the powerful German army. By 1940, France was under German control. Hitler was making plans to invade Britain.

First, he had to win control of the skies above Britain. The Battle of Britain was the first real air battle in history. German and British planes fought for three months, but the Germans couldn't defeat the British airmen. Finally, like Napoleon before him, Hitler chose to invade Russia, not Britain. And like Napoleon's, his invasion failed.

The US was now fighting on the same side as Britain, and together they pushed the Germans out of France. At the same time the Russians were pushing the Germans back through the countries of Eastern Europe. By May 1945, Germany was defeated and Hitler was dead.

But the war in Asia continued. Japan joined Germany in the war in 1941 and took control of many British lands in Asia. A quarter of a million British and American soldiers and ordinary people were made prisoners by the Japanese. But the Americans finally defeated the Japanese in the Pacific Ocean. The British pushed them out of Burma and India. In August 1945, Japan was defeated.

Winston Churchill

Churchill was from an important family of lords and politicians and he joined Parliament at the age of 25. In the 1930s, he realised before most people in Britain that Hitler was very dangerous. When the Second World War began, he soon became head of the government. Because of his powerful speeches in the most difficult months of the war, the British started to believe that they could win. Churchill played a very important part in the war against Hitler.

The end of the Empire

After the Second World War, Britain couldn't keep control of its empire. India and Pakistan became independent in 1947, and most other countries in the empire soon followed. Hong Kong stayed British for a much longer time, but in 1997 it became part of China.

When the countries of the Empire became independent, most of them joined the Commonwealth. This is a group of states that work together on many important matters, like business, health and the fight against poverty. The British queen is still the head of the Commonwealth.

Britain's place in the world today

Britain is part of the Commonwealth and the European Union and, as a result of its history and language, it works closely with the US too. Britain's days of world power have ended, but it is still richer and more powerful than most countries in the world.

Without its empire, Britain is a small country again – but a small country with a big history.

ACTIVITIES

Chapter 1

Before you read

1 How many famous people from British history can you name? Write a list, and then compare your list with the lists of other students. Have you got the same names?

2 Look at the Word List at the back of the book. Discuss the answers to these questions. What do you think?
   a Has your country ever fought in a battle against Britain? Has it ever fought on the same side? What was the battle about? What happened?
   b Did any foreign armies invade and conquer Britain in the 20th century? Was Britain invaded before that?

3 Look at the Timeline on page vi. Can you find answers to 2b (above)?

While you read

4 In what order did these people arrive in Britain? Number them, 1–6.
   a People from India and the Caribbean   . . . .
   b The Vikings   . . . .
   c The Romans   . . . .
   d The Normans   . . . .
   e The Angles and Saxons   . . . .
   f Protestants from France and the Netherlands . . . .

After you read

5 Did these people make a big difference to British history? Why (not)? What did they do?
   King Harold   Boudica   Alfred the Great
   William the Conqueror

6 Work in pairs. Have this conversation.
   Student A: Imagine that you are with William the Conqueror in 1076. Ask him questions about his conquest of England.
   Student B: Imagine that you are William the Conqueror in 1076. Answer the questions.

Chapter 2

Before you read

7 Discuss these questions.
   a What are the names of the four countries in the United Kingdom?
   b What are the capital cities of these countries?

While you read

8 Are these sentences right (R) or wrong (W)?
   a After 1603, England and Scotland had different kings. . . . .
   b England, Wales and Scotland became one state in 1707. . . . .
   c Most Irish people in the 16th century were Catholic. . . . .
   d A lot of Irish people died in the 1840s because they became Protestant. . . . .
   e Part of Ireland is still in the United Kingdom. . . . .
   f The parliament in London has no power in Scotland and Wales now. . . . .

After you read

9 Imagine that you are an Irish Catholic in the 1850s. You want independence from Britain. Explain why.
10 There are four small countries in the state of the United Kingdom. Is it good for countries to join together in this way? Think about wars, trade, languages, and the ideas of the people in the smaller countries in the state.

Chapter 3

Before you read

11 This chapter describes how Britain became a Protestant country. Answer the questions.
   a Do you know any differences between Catholic and Protestant ideas about religion?
   b Why do you think Britain first became Protestant?

12 Were these people Catholic or Protestant at the end of their time as king/queen? Write C or P.

  a Henry VIII ....

  b Edward VI ....

  c Mary I ....

  d Elizabeth I ....

  e Mary Queen of Scots ....

  f James II ....

After you read

13 How were these people important to religion in Britain?
  Katharine of Aragon   Anne Boleyn   Thomas Wolsey
  King Philip of Spain

14 In what ways were Mary I and Elizabeth I similar? In what ways were they different?

Chapter 4

Before you read

15 In this chapter you are going to read about disagreements between kings and politicians. First answer these questions.

  a Does Britain have a king or a queen today?

  b Which is more powerful now, the king/queen or Parliament?

While you read

16 Join the two halves of the sentences.

  a John   was killed because of his
                                  disagreements with Parliament.

  b Ordinary businessmen   ruled Britain as Lord Protector.

  c Charles I   gave the control of Britain to
                                  Parliament.

  d Oliver Cromwell   were in the first parliament.

  e William and Mary   were asked by Parliament to
                                  rule Britain.

  f George I   agreed to a list of rules for
                                  good government.

After you read

17 Imagine you are judging Charles I in court. Should he live or should he die? Why?

18 Do you think it's good for a country to have a king or queen? Why (not)?

Chapter 5

Before you read

19 Do you think these sentences are right or wrong? Guess your answers, then read the chapter and check.

a New ideas for farms in the 18th century made life better for everyone.

b Britain's first factories didn't make anyone rich.

c Some towns with big populations had no politicians at the start of the 19th century.

d Workers' lives got better without a revolution like the one in France.

While you read

20 In what order did these changes happen? Number them, 1–6.

a Cloth was made in factories.	....
b All women over 21 could vote.	....
c Hospitals and doctors were free.	....
d All men over 21 could vote.	....
e Children couldn't work 18-hour days.	....
f All children had to go to school.	....

After you read

21 Work in pairs. Imagine that you both work in a factory in the early 19th century. Have a discussion.

Student A: You want to ask the owner of your factory for more pay. If he doesn't agree, you'll refuse to work.

Student B: You agree that the pay is very low. But you don't want to lose your job. You have a lot of young children.

Chapter 6

Before you read

22 Does/did your country have an empire? Do you know which
countries were part of the British Empire?

While you read

23 Write the names. Use a different name for each question.

    a a country that became independent from Britain in 1776

      ....

    b a country where British criminals were sent

      ....

    c a battle in which Britain won control of the seas

      ....

    d a French ruler who almost invaded Britain

      ....

    e a British politician who was important in defeating Hitler

      ....

    f a place that became part of China in 1997

      ....

After you read

24 Are/were these people friends or enemies of the British
Government?

    a the people who sailed to America in the Mayflower

    b the American Indians

    c the East India Company

    d the ruler of Bengal

    e Horatio Nelson

    f the Germans in the First World War

    g the Americans in the Second World War

    h the countries of the Commonwealth today

Writing

25 Choose a subject in British history for a demonstration (for example,
votes for women, Irish independence, better pay in factories). Write
to a newspaper explaining the reasons for your demonstration.

26 There is going to be a TV programme about the greatest person from British history. Write to the programme makers. Tell them about one person who should be in the programme. Give reasons.

27 You are a filmmaker. Write a short description of your film about a time in British history.

28 You are a soldier at the start of a war or battle in British history. Write a letter to your family. Explain why the armies are fighting. Describe what will probably happen in the future.

29 Choose an important day in British history. Write a newspaper report about it.

30 You work for the 'Time Travel Talk Show'. Choose a guest for the show and write a list of ten questions for him/her.

31 You are a historian. Write the Introduction to your book about a king or queen of Britain.

32 You are an ordinary person who is living at a time of great change in Britain. Decide which time that is. Write a letter to a friend. Describe how your life has changed in the past year.